Amaz

Amazon Echo For Beginners

Everything You Need To Know About Amazon Echo Now

Table Of Contents

Introduction

When Amazon finally launched Echo, everyone has basically the same sentiments—it indeed is a hint of what the future holds. It solidifies the notion that there is indeed great things you can do with a smart home, which Echo and Alexa has made possible. There are so many things you can do with the device, and this book you will find out about the Amazon Echo and its features.

This book is all about the Amazon Echo and the Alexa. However, you will also learn something about the related devices such as the Amazon Echo Dot and the Amazon Tap. You'll learn about how Amazon Echo works. You will also learn about the functionalities of other similar devices.

We'll start by giving you some insight on the history and early days of the device as well as a brief overview of its operation and services, just so you'd have an idea of just how it's supposed to work. You'll also get an idea on the implications of its usage and further development of the technology.

And because the Amazon Echo is not perfect, we'll also tell you about the limitations and common issues and concerns that users have when using the device.

If you have just purchased the Amazon Echo and you have no idea on how to use it, this book is especially recommended. It is written with beginner users in mind. It contains vital information about the manufacture of the Amazon Echo, the features of the device, and the things that you can try with it.

Furthermore, this book gives you detailed and easy to follow instructions to help you make the most of your Amazon Echo. It tells you how you can set up the device and what commands you can use on it. It also tells you about the differences between the Amazon Echo, Amazon Echo Dot, and Amazon Tap.

Let's begin the journey.

Chapter 1: What Is the Amazon Echo?

The Amazon Echo is a wireless speaker and voice command tool. The device is available in cylinder form and is about nine inches tall and three inches wide. It features a speaker and seven microphones that are specifically made to listen for the "wake word" of the Echo and respond to the commands of the user. It answers to the name "Alexa." After all, it is powered by the Alexa software. Nevertheless, the user can change the wake word to either Echo or Amazon.

The Amazon Echo is capable of a lot of things, such as music playback, voice interaction, streaming podcasts, setting alarms, providing traffic and weather information in real time, and playing audio books. It can even control certain smart devices and serve as a home automation hub.

The Echo has been in development since 2010 and now, it is finally here. It is actually part of the company's initial efforts to broaden their device portfolio. Amazon is best known for its Kindle e-book reader; but now that the Echo is here, its popularity has soared even higher. The Amazon Echo was featured in the 2016 Super Bowl ads.

At first, the Amazon Echo was limited to members of Amazon Prime only. It can also be accessed by people who were invited to access it. Nevertheless, in June 23, 2015, the device has been introduced to the American public. Since then, the Amazon Echo has been one of the most talked about devices in the United States.

What's more, rumor has it that the Amazon Echo is about to make its debut in Canada in the middle or latter part of 2016. This speculation was the result of Amazon posting job listings for software developers in Canada. The company even took part in a hackathon there.

Even better, the Alexa voice service can be incorporated into a variety of devices. Amazon even encourages people to connect the services and devices of other companies to the Echo.

Operation Overview

By default, the Amazon Echo continually listens to speech and waits for the user to say the wake word. So basically, it remains on stand-by mode until the user mentions the wake word, and then it comes to life.

In addition, the Amazon Echo has a remote control that can both be voice-activated and manually-activated. This remote control may be used in place of the wake word. So if you are the user, you can take control of the Amazon Echo using your remote control. There is no more need for you to mention the wake word in order for it to function according to what you want.

The device's microphones can be disabled manually. You just have to press the mute button if you wish to turn the audio processing circuit off. Then again, you have to keep in mind that Wi-Fi is necessary in order for the Amazon Echo to work. If you do not have a Wi-Fi connection, you will not be able to use the device.

With regard to the voice recognition capability of the Amazon Echo, it is actually based on the Web Services and common voice platform of Amazon, which it obtained from IVONA, Yap, and Evi.

If you have a good Internet connection or an Internet connection with low latency, then there is good news for you because the Amazon Echo performs nicely in this kind of situation. It actually reduces the processing time because there are much fewer communication round trips, geo-distributed service endpoints, and streamable responses.

Services Offered

The Amazon Echo offers a variety of services that you may find useful. For instance, it offers weather reports from AccuWeather as well as news reports from various sources, including ESPN, NPN, and radio stations.

The Amazon Echo is capable of playing music. Good for you if you have an Amazon Music account because your Echo can play your songs. Nevertheless, it is alright if you do not have an Amazon Music account because your Echo can still play songs and music from Apple Music, Google Play, and other streaming services. So, you can play the songs and audio files that you have on your tablet or smartphone.

The device also offers support for Spotify and Pandora. Likewise, it offers support for Nest Thermostats and IFTTT. Moreover, it has voice-controlled alarms, to-do lists, shopping lists, and timers. It can even access articles on the Wikipedia website. The device responds to every question thrown at it with regard to the items found in the Google calendar.

The Amazon Echo is also integrated with Philips Hue, Yonomi, SmartThings, Belkin Wemo, Wink, and Insteon. Currently, Amazon is working to integrate the Echo with more systems, such as Mojio, MARA, Toymail, Scout Alarm, Orange Chef, and Garageio.

That's not all. The device is also capable of doing other things, thanks to the Alexa Skills Kit. Actually, these are third-party developed voice experiences that make the Echo much more functional. So, you can make your Echo answer questions, play music, set alarms, call an Uber car, and even order pizza from your favorite pizza place.

The Alexa Skills Kit is actually a compilation of code samples, documentations, and API tools that make it easy and quick for developers to add more skills to the Alexa. The developers can even make use of the Smart Home Skill API, which is a pleasant addition to the collection.

The Smart Home Skill API can teach the Alexa how to take control of thermostat devices and cloud-controlled lighting fixtures. Every code involved works in the cloud, and not on the user device. Developers can also refer to tutorials if they want to know how they can quickly create voice experiences for both existing and new applications.

Voice System and Software Updates

The Amazon Echo is unlike any other devices that have a robot-like voice. Its realistic voice is the result of a speech-unit selection technology. Specialized natural language processing (NLP) algorithms are used to produce high speech accuracy. These algorithms can be found in the text-to-speech (TTS) engine of the Amazon Echo.

With regard to the functionality of the device, it evolves periodically as the company produces new software. A lot of the more recent releases are actually able to repair bugs aside from their already enhanced functionalities.

There are new releases being pushed gradually. Thus, it can take a few days or even weeks for certain devices to get updates. Due to the fact that most of the Amazon Echo's intelligence relies on the cloud, certain improvements can be done to the device without having to update the software program that it runs on. For instance, in April 2015, the Amazon Echo had the new capability of giving live sports score updates. The developers did not have to update its current software to add this functionality.

Hardware and Connectivity

The hardware of the Amazon Echo includes 4GB storage space, a DM3725 ARM Cortex-A8 processor from Texas Instruments, and 256MB LPDDR1 RAM. The device connects with Bluetooth 4.0 and dual-band Wi-Fi 802.11 a/b/g/n.

Input and Related Gadgets

The Amazon Echo is designed and developed to be controlled by the human voice, although users can also find a microphone enabled remote control to be used on it. There is an action button at the top part of the unit, which allows the user to setup in different locations. There is also a mute button that allows the user to turn off his microphones. The volume of the speaker can be increased or decreased by rotating the device's top half-inch part. Keep in mind that the Amazon Echo does not have any internal battery, so you have to plug it in if you want to use it.

In March 2016, the Amazon Echo Dot was introduced by Amazon. It is actually a mini version of the Amazon Echo. Its design is similar to a hockey puck. It is meant to be connected to the speakers because it has a tiny speaker. It also allows the user to use the functions that are similar to the Amazon Echo. There is another mini version of the Amazon Echo and that is the Amazon Tap. It has dual stereo speakers.

Concerns Regarding Privacy

The Amazon Echo raises some concerns with regard to privacy. Users are citing issues regarding the access of the Amazon Echo to private discussions in homes, as well as non-verbal signs that allow the user to determine who is inside the home. Users can find out who is inside the house because of audible indications like television and radio programs, and footstep-cadence.

The company responded to these issues by saying that the Amazon Echo merely streams recordings that come from the home of the user whenever the wake word is uttered and the device is activated. Nonetheless, the Amazon Echo is still able to stream voice recordings. It is actually listening to everything in order to be alerted when the user says the wake word.

The Amazon Echo makes use of the previous voice recordings that the user has uploaded to the cloud in order to improve the responses to possible questions that may arise in the future. In order to address any concerns with regard to privacy, the user has the options to delete his voice recordings in his account.

However, it should be kept in mind that doing this can diminish the total user experience with regard to the voice search feature of the Amazon Echo. Anyway, if you wish to delete a voice recording, you just have to go to your *Manage My Device* page on the official site of Amazon or contact customer service for assistance.

The Amazon Echo makes use of an address that has been set in the Alexa companion application whenever it needs to access a particular location. The company, along with websites and third-party applications, makes use of location information in order to offer useful services. They also do this to store information and offer voice services, *Find Your Device*, and the *Maps* application. They also observe the accuracy and performance of their services.

For instance, the Amazon Echo voice services can use your location in order to give in to your request of searching for nearby stores, spas, restaurants, or any other establishments. Likewise, the Amazon Echo relies on your location in order to process your requests as well as enhance your Maps experience. Keep in mind that every piece of information gathered is bound by the Privacy Notice of Amazon.

The company keeps the digital recordings of the users' spoken audio after they mention their wake up word. Even though these audio recordings are subject to the demands of government agents, law enforcement, and other entities through subpoena, the company still publishes information regarding the warrants that it gets, as well as the subpoenas and other warrant-less demands that it receives. This allows the customers to have an idea or insight with regard to the illegal demand percentage for the customer information that it gets.

Limitations

If you wish to purchase digital media or merchandise, such as songs, you have to command the Amazon Echo to do it. However, you have to do some manual interventions via the alternate user interface in order for you to be able to complete your purchase. The Amazon Echo has shown hit or miss results whenever it was asked certain questions that users wanted better answers to. Even more, the Amazon Echo sometimes makes a mistake when it comes to homophones.

At present, the location of the Amazon Echo is set to Seattle, which is also the headquarters of the company. This location is set by default. If you wish to change it, you have to do it manually. Then again, you can only change its location to somewhere within the country. You cannot change it to any other location outside of the United States.

You should take note that this is not the same as the smartphone-based voice assistant that actually gets the precise location through the GPS locators that are built into the device. Such restriction may result in incorrect information or answers to questions about locations, such as asking about the weather in a particular location. The Amazon Echo may also make a mistake when it comes to setting an alarm for a certain local time that is not in your location.

Nevertheless, there have been attempts to get through such limitations. For instance, there are users who set the Amazon Echo with exactly twelve hours difference in time zones. For instance, if it is 11:30 AM in London, you can set your Amazon

Echo to 11:30 PM, which is the Hawaii Standard Time. Doing so will enable your device to give you the correct time.

Then again, this method is not perfect. In fact, it can have a couple of unpleasant effects. For instance, you can get a wrong AM and PM notation. You can also get a wrong date. You can also manipulate the information that the device transmits and receives. If you use this more complex method, you can get more desirable and accurate results. However, you need to have adequate technical skills. You also need to use the Request Maker for Google Chrome in order for you to be successful at using this method.

Furthermore, you may not be thrilled to find out that the communication and interaction with the Amazon Echo can only be done in English. There are no other languages available.

Chapter 2: Setting It Up

The Amazon Echo is very easy to setup. It is so easy that it will merely take you a few minutes to get things done. You just need to plug the speaker in, download and run the Alexa application, and do things according to the prompts that appear. Even though it is a Bluetooth speaker, the Amazon Echo still connects to the Wi-Fi networks in the homes of the users in order to process their voice commands over the Internet.

This is actually pretty useful especially if you listen to audio files and music using the embedded applications of the speakers. Amazon uses the term "skills" to refer to these embedded applications. Do not worry because the sound does not cut out when the phone gets out of range. You will still be able to listen to your music without any interruption.

The Amazon Echo also has an application that requires users to log in using their Amazon user accounts. In this case, you need to setup your Amazon account to be able to link the speaker to everything that you purchased for the past years using Amazon. So, if you purchased some e-books or music a couple of years ago, you will still be able to access them through your Amazon Echo.

Connecting the Amazon Echo to Wi-Fi Hotspots

If you are at home, it is best if you have a Wi-Fi hotspot in which you can connect the Amazon Echo to. It could even be a pocket Wi-Fi; it does not really matter so long as you can connect. However, if you are not home, you can still connect your device to your mobile phone and use this gadget as your Wi-Fi hotspot. So, you see, you can actually use the Amazon Echo anywhere.

Before you can connect the Amazon Echo to any Wi-Fi hotspot though, you'll need to get the most recent software version for the device. It should be 3389 or higher. You also need to have the Alexa application on a mobile device that is supported by the software, such as an Android or iOS. In addition, you need to have a mobile service plan that supports your Wi-Fi hotspot.

Keep in mind that when you set up the Amazon Echo for the very first time, you may not have the choice to connect it to a mobile hotspot. So, in order for you to be able to connect it to a mobile hotspot, you need to download and install the most recent software and enable the feature. When you do that, you should be able to connect the Amazon Echo to the Wi-Fi network in your home.

So, how can you connect the Amazon Echo to a Wi-Fi hotspot?

First, you need to go to the settings menu on your smartphone or mobile device. Then, you have to look for an option for the Wi-Fi hotspot. Once you find one, take note of the password and network name for the hotspot.

Go to your Alexa application and open the left navigation panel on your screen. Go to *Settings* and choose your Amazon Echo device. Choose the option *Update Wi-Fi*.

Then, you have to look for the Action button your Amazon Echo and press and hold it for about five seconds. When you do that, you should see the light ring turning orange. If you see this happening, it means that your Amazon Echo is connecting with a

Wi-Fi network. You should also be able to see a list of the available networks in your location in the app.

Take note that the Alexa app might ask you to connect the Amazon Echo manually through the settings.

Anyway, you should scroll downward until you see the option Use this device as a Wi-Fi hotspot. When you see that, select it. Then, choose Start.

Input the name of the network as well as the password for the hotspot. Then, choose Connect and see to it that you input all the necessary network information properly. In case you entered the wrong network information, the Amazon Echo will not connect to the Wi-Fi hotspot in your home.

Next, you should go to the settings menu on your phone and turn on the Wi-Fi hotspot. The Amazon Echo searches for the Wi-Fit hotspot in devices. So, the moment it connects to the hotspot of your phone, Alexa confirms that the connection is successful and you can now use the device.

Keep in mind that each time you use your mobile device to function as a Wi-Fi hotspot, the Amazon Echo uses the data connection of your device. As a result, you may incur additional charges from your service provider. However, this would still depend on your chosen data plan. You should call the hotline of your service provider in case you have any questions or you wish to know more information with regard to the additional charges.

Connecting the Amazon Echo to Wi-Fi

The Amazon Echo needs to connect to an active Wi-Fi network in order for it to function and follow your commands. It will not be able to stream media, speak, and follow your commands if it is not connected to a Wi-Fi network.

Anyway, before you start to use your Amazon Echo, see to it that you plug it into a power outlet. As you have read previously, it does not have any batteries. So, you need to plug it into a power outlet each time you want to use it. You may also want to invest in a power generator in case the power runs out and you want to continue using your Amazon Echo.

Once you have plugged your Amazon Echo in, just open your Alexa application and run it. Take note that the Amazon Echo makes use of a dual-band Wi-Fi (2.4 GHz / 5 GHz) networks, which in turn make use of the 802.11 a / b / g / n standard. The Amazon Echo doesn't connect to any peer-to-peer or ad-hoc networks.

Once you go to your Alexa app, open your left navigation panel on your screen. Then, choose *Settings* and choose the device that you want to use. Next, choose *Update Wi-Fi*. In case you wish to add another device to your account, you have to choose *Set up a new device* rather than *Update Wi-Fi*.

Once you go to your Amazon Echo device, look for the Action button and then press and hold it for about five seconds. You should see that its light ring turns into an orange color. You should also notice that your device starts to connect to your Amazon Echo device. In addition, you should be able to see the list of the Wi-Fi networks in your area. This list should show up on the application.

Once again, you have to take note that the Alexa app may require you to connect your Amazon Echo with your mobile device manually. You can do this via the settings of your Wi-Fi.

Choose a Wi-Fi network and then input your password if necessary. In case you do not see the Wi-Fi network on the list, just continue scrolling down. Then, you have to choose *Add a Network* or *Rescan*. You should only choose *Add a Network*, however, if your network is hidden.

Be mindful of the MAC address in case you have to add the Alexa device to the list of approved devices of your router. If this is the case, scroll down on your screen until you see your MAC address.

You may want to save the password of your Wi-Fi to Amazon, but this is purely optional. You may or may not do it at all. Keep in mind that the Wi-Fi passwords that you save while you set up your device instantly show up each time you connect another device to your Wi-Fi network. When you change between saved networks, your password also gets remembered.

Connecting to public networks is also another option, but it is purely optional as well. You may input the necessary information if you want to connect to public networks that require users to sign into their Web browser. You may find public networks in hotels, airports, or schools.

The information you may need to input can be your room number, a pre-determined password, or simply a button that affirms your acceptance of their terms and policies for using their public network. Unlike the previous information mentioned, however, this kind of information can't be saved on your Amazon account.

Finally, you should choose Connect and wait for your device to connect to your selected Wi-Fi network. When the connection is successful, you would see a confirmation message in your application. When this happens, you can start using the Alexa.

Pairing Mobile Devices with the Amazon Echo

The Amazon Echo is Bluetooth-enabled, which means that you can stream audio services, such as Google Play Music and iTunes from your tablet, phone, or any other mobile devices.

Anyway, before you start, see to it that you set the mode of the mobile device to Bluetooth pairing. This way, it would be ready to connect to the available device of your choice. In addition, you should see to it that your mobile device is within range of the Amazon Echo. If it is too far away, the Amazon Echo will not be able to detect the mobile device.

You have to take note that text messages, phone calls, and any other notifications coming from the mobile device are not read and cannot be received by the Amazon Echo. Likewise, any audio coming from the Amazon Echo cannot be sent to your Bluetooth speakers and headphones.

When you are ready to pair your mobile device with your Amazon Echo, you should utter the word "Pair" and Alexa will prepare to connect. Then again, if you wish to exit the Bluetooth pairing mode because you changed your mind or you have any other reason, you simply have to utter the word "Cancel" and the setup will come to a halt.

Go to the Bluetooth settings menu of the mobile device and open it. When you are there, you should choose your Amazon Echo device. Alexa will let you know if the connection is a success. If it is, you can now stream audio from your mobile device to your Amazon Echo.

If you wish to disconnect the mobile device from the Amazon Echo, you simply have to utter the word "Disconnect". Keep in mind that once you pair the mobile device with the Amazon Echo device, you can instantly connect them together. You have to turn on the Bluetooth on the mobile device and utter the word "Connect". If the Amazon Echo is connected to multiple mobile devices, you will notice that it connects to the one that is most recently paired with it.

What are the Supported Bluetooth Profiles of the Amazon Echo?

It is necessary for the mobile device to have a supported profile to be paired with the Amazon Echo. As you have read earlier, Alexa neither reads nor receives text messages, phone calls, and other notifications coming from mobile devices. The Amazon Echo is not capable of sending audio to Bluetooth speakers and headphones. In addition, Mac OS X devices, such as the MacBook Air does not support hands-free voice control.

The Advanced Audio Distribution Profile or A2DP is a supported Bluetooth profile and it allows the user to stream audio files from his mobile device, such as tablet or smartphone, to the Amazon Echo.

The Audio / Video Remote Control Profile or AVRCP is another supported Bluetooth profile and it allows the user to make use of a hands-free voice control whenever a mobile device gets connected to the Amazon Echo.

Chapter 3: Alexa Support

The Alexa Voice Service is actually a cloud-based service that powers the various products that are enabled by Alexa. These products include the Amazon Echo as well as other products that the Amazon Company does not produce.

If you wish to use Alexa on products that are Alexa-enabled, you have to set up the device or product first. When you are done setting it up, you have to connect it to the Internet. See to it that you follow the instructions of the manufacturer carefully in order to avoid any issues or problems. You may also want to check out their official website or refer to their product companion application for more details.

Once you reach the product companion application or website, sign in using your Amazon account in order to enable the Alexa.

You also have to download the Alexa application in order for you to be able to manage your settings, such as Smart Home and Music and Media among others.

Next, open your Alexa application to make a request. Once you are done with your request, you should test it out. Take note that there are some Alexa-enabled products that may not support every Alexa feature. When you go to your Alexa application, you may notice some features or settings that are not supported by the other Alexa-enabled products.

Keep in mind that the Alexa functions independently on Alexa-enabled devices. Nonetheless, there are still certain settings and content that is shared among devices.

The Alexa application can be used on iOS, Android, Fire OS, and various desktop browsers. Through this application, you can manage your settings. Alexa will let you configure the settings of your Alexa-enabled products, gain access to your dialog history, configure your alarms and timers, check out your to-do list and shopping list, identify and enable any third-party skills, identify and set up your smart home devices, and learn more about Things to Try.

If you encounter any issues and you need help in setting up the device, connecting to the Internet, activating the Alexa, or fixing issues related to device-specific skills and supported Alexa features, call the manufacturer of your device.

What are the Differences between the Amazon Echo, Amazon Echo Dot, and Amazon Tap?

All of these three products are created by Amazon and all three of them have access to the Alexa Voice Service. Then again, even though they seem the same, they are all different devices.

In this part of this chapter, you will learn about the main differences between these three devices. For starters, when it comes to portability, only the Amazon Tap is portable. The Amazon Echo and the Amazon Echo Dot are not portable, so you cannot take them with you wherever you go. This is mainly because they are not powered by batteries and you have to plug them into a power outlet each time you wish to use them.

With regard to power, both the Amazon Echo and the Amazon Echo Dot require a power adapter to function whereas the Amazon Tap requires a non-removable but rechargeable battery.

When it comes to Wi-Fi, all three devices require 802.11 a/b/g/n. The Amazon Echo and the Amazon Echo Dot are dual-band while the Amazon Tap is single-band.

All three devices run on the Alexa software, but the Amazon Echo and the Amazon Echo Dot can be activated using a wake word while the Amazon Tap can be activated by using the microphone button.

The Amazon Echo and the Amazon Echo Dot are basically like twins, with the Echo Dot being the smaller twin. However, when it comes to speakers, the two devices actually differ. The Amazon Echo has mono speakers while the Amazon Echo Dot has stereo speakers, just like the Amazon Tap.

Both the Amazon Echo and the Amazon Echo Dot does not feature the Dolby Audio, but the Amazon Tap does. Also, the Amazon Echo and the Amazon Echo Dot has Light Ring, Action button, and Mute button for buttons and lights while the Amazon Tap has front light indicators and power, microphone, Wi-Fi, Bluetooth, and dedicated playback buttons.

With regard to the Bluetooth Audio Input feature, all three devices have it. However, only the Amazon Echo Dot has a Bluetooth Audio Output; the Amazon Echo and the Amazon Tap does not have it.

When it comes to the AUX Audio Input, only the Amazon Tap has it. However, only the Amazon Echo Dot has the AUX Audio Output feature. Are the devices compatible with the Voice Remote feature of the Amazon Echo? Both the Amazon Echo and the Amazon Echo Dot are compatible with it, but the Amazon Tap is not.

How about the accessories involved? The Amazon Echo features a Voice Remote, which is sold separately. The Amazon Tap has an inclusive Charging Cradle, but its Amazon Tap Sling is sold separately. The Amazon Echo Dot has an inclusive 3.5 mm audio cable, but its Voice Remote is sold separately. Obviously, you need to purchase the accessories that are not included in the package if you wish to have them.

Sadly, the Amazon Echo, the Amazon Tap, and the Amazon Echo Dot do not have any media storage. Nonetheless, they all have the Alexa application, so that is still good news for users.

What Are the Features Supported by Alexa?

There are certain Alexa features that are not supported by certain Alexa devices. Nonetheless, you will be glad to know that all the Alexa features of Amazon Echo devices, such as the Echo and the Echo Dot, are supported. Likewise, the Alexa features of Alexa-enabled Amazon devices, such as the Amazon Tap are supported.

How about Fire TV devices? If you want to use the Alexa on a Fire TV device, you have to use the Voice Remote for Amazon Fire TV as well as the Amazon Fire TV Remote application or the Fire TV Stick.

Keep in mind that the supported features of Alexa are all the same on all the Fire TV devices. Then again, some of the features are currently not available for use, such as timers and alarms, Bluetooth voice control, Spotify Premium, volume control via voice commands, voice training, Voicecast, and smart home devices that do not have a hub.

The Alexa is available on certain third-party products. If you wish to find out which of the features of Alexa are supported on your device, you have to check out the website from which you got your device.

Changing the Wake Word

If you wish to communicate with your Amazon Echo, you simply have to utter your wake word. As you have learned, you can use the words "Alexa", "Amazon", and "Echo" as your wake words. You just have to choose one.

Anyway, if it is your first time to use the Amazon Echo and you want to change its wake word, you need to open your Alexa application and go to the left navigation panel. You would see *Settings*. Select it and look for your device on the menu.

Once you see your device, you have to select it as well, and then scroll downwards to choose *Wake Word*. Then, choose a wake word from your drop-down menu. Once you are done with that, you just have to save it. You know that you have successfully changed your wake word when you see the light ring on your Amazon Echo flashing orange lights.

Talking to Your Alexa Device

The Alexa actually works across several devices and recalls each and every one of your preferences. Once you have activated the Alexa, you can start commanding it to do tasks or you can start asking questions.

How do you activate the Alexa on a variety of devices?

If you are using the Amazon Echo or the Amazon Echo Dot, you have to utter your wake word before you say your command, request, or question.

If you are using the Amazon Tap, just press and then release the microphone button, also referred to as the talk button, before you utter your command, request, or question. There is no need for you to hold down the talk button or the microphone button. There is no need for you to utter the wake word either. If the Alexa requests for a reply, there is no need for you to press the talk button or the microphone button again.

If you are using a Fire TV device, you have to press down and hold the microphone button on your Fire TV Remote app or Fire TV Voice Remote before you utter your command, request, or question. When you are done saying what you want to say, you can release the microphone button. There is no need for you to utter the wake word when you say your command or request.

Using Multiple Alexa Devices

The Alexa functions independently on Alexa-enabled devices. There are certain settings and content that are shared. Keep in mind that you are allowed to manage up to twelve Alexa devices in the Alexa application, provided that these devices are registered in your Amazon account.

Every Alexa device is controlled independently via voice or the Alexa application. It is not possible to connect multiple Alexa devices with one another and play the same audio file at the same time. This is actually a good thing because the users who share the connection can make different requests or play different audio files and music without being an interruption to another user.

In case you have more than one device, you can make each one of your devices respond separately and do the tasks that you ordered to be done.

For instance, if you are using the Amazon Echo and the Amazon Echo Dot at the same time, you have to choose two different wake words for each of them. This is especially crucial if the two devices are very near or within speaking range of each other.

If, in any case, you cannot or do not want to change the wake words of your devices, you need to separate them. You actually need to put them in different rooms and they have to be far away enough from each other so that they will not interact.

You have to put your devices that share the same wake word in separate rooms. As much as possible, they have to be at least thirty feet apart from each other. You have to use your Voice Remote for Amazon Echo, which is sold separately, in order for you to be able to communicate with a specific device.

If you are using Amazon Tap and a Fire TV device, there is no more need for you to utter the wake word before you utter your request or command. You just have to give your devices distinct names.

How about common settings and shared content?

In case you own two or more Alexa devices that are registered to your account, you may share some of your settings and content between your devices. You just have to go to the settings menu of your Alexa application and then go to the Account section. You will notice that every item in this section is the same for each and every one of your Alexa devices, such as shopping list, to-do list, flash briefing, smart home devices, household profiles, and music and media.

There are also certain content that is not common between the devices on a similar account, such as timers and alarms, sounds, wake word, and Bluetooth connections among others. Unfortunately, you are currently not allowed to customize the content that you want to be available on your device.

Pairing the Amazon Echo Remote

You have the option to use or not use this accessory for your Amazon Echo. However, you have to keep in mind that you can only use one remote for your Amazon Echo at a time. The Amazon Echo Remote is actually compatible with the Echo and the Echo Dot. It is not included in the package when you purchase the Amazon Echo, though. You need to order and pay for it separately.

You need to pull down the latch on the battery door of your remote, and then you have to pull it away from it. Next, you need to insert a couple of AAA batteries, which are included in the package, into your remote. You need to replace the battery door, of course. See to it that your batteries are in their proper orientations.

When you go to your Alexa app, you need to open the navigation menu, which is found at the left side. Then, you have to choose *Settings* and select the Amazon Echo device that you are using. You need to choose *Pair Remote* to pair the two devices together.

You may notice *Forget Remote* showing up in your app. When this happens, you can tell that there is already a remote that is paired with your device. If you are replacing the remote, you have to choose *Forget Remote* first. When you are done with that, you can now pair another remote with the device.

Press down and hold the *Play / Pause* button on your remote for about five seconds before releasing it. The device will search for the remote and connect with it within forty seconds. This time may be longer, though. It may take longer than forty seconds for the device to search and connect with the remote. Nevertheless, once the device successfully finds the remote, you will hear Alexa say "Your remote has been paired."

Using Voice Control for Paired Devices

Once you have successfully paired your mobile device, such as your tablet or phone, with your Alexa device, you can now make use of voice control as you listen to audiobooks, music, and other audio files.

You have to keep in mind, however, that the voice control feature is not available for the Mac OS X. So, if you are using MacBook Air or other similar devices, you cannot use this feature.

Anyway, if you want to use voice control for your device, you have to utter the word "Connect" in order for the Alexa to search for your mobile device and connect with it immediately.

You also need to open a media or music app on your mobile device so you can choose a track. This track will play on your Alexa device. If you want to control the playback feature on the Alexa device, you have to use certain voice commands such as play, previous, pause, next, resume, stop, and restart.

In case you request a particular album, artist, song, or playlist while you listen to the audio on your mobile device, Alexa will halt or pause the playback on your gadget and disconnect from it promptly. The music you have on your Amazon Music library will play instead. If you want to play music via Bluetooth, you have to press the play button on your mobile device and request for Alexa to connect.

Issues Commonly Experienced with the Alexa App

Just like many other great apps out there, users have also reported certain issues with the Alexa.

The Alexa Application Does Not Work

Have you ever tried to use the Alexa only to find out that it is not working at all? If you cannot open the application or you are getting an error message saying that the application is offline, you may have issues with compatibility.

You have to remember that the Alexa application is not compatible with everything. It is only compatible with Android 4.4 or higher, iOS 7.0 or higher, Fire OS 2.0 or higher, and certain Web browsers, such as Internet Explorer 10 or higher, Google Chrome, Mozilla Firefox, Safari, and Microsoft Edge.

If you are on iOS, you may have to restart your device, whether it is an iPhone, iPod touch, or iPad. You have to press down and hold the *Sleep / Wake* button until you see a slider show up on your screen. Once you see this slider, you have to press it and drag it in order for the device to be turned off. When your gadget has been turned off, you have to press down and hold the *Sleep / Wake* button and restart it.

In some cases, you may need to force close your application. How can you do this? First, you need to press down the *Home* button two times until you see the preview of your most recently used applications. These applications will show up on your screen. When you see them, you have to swipe them until you see your Alexa application. Then, you have to swipe up and close the app.

You can also just uninstall and then reinstall the application. This usually works for users who have done the two methods stated above and still did not get their expected results. To do this method, you need to press down and hold the Alexa application until you see it shake on your screen. Then, you have to tap on the "x" icon on the application to uninstall it. Once you have successfully removed it from your device, you have to go to the Apple App Store and get the Alexa app once more. Of course, you have to install it the same way you did the first time you had it on your device.

If you are an Android user, you may have to restart your device. To do so, you simply have to press down and hold the *Power* button. Then, you have to choose the option that allows you to turn the device off. Once you have turned off your device, you need to press down the *Power* button once more so that you can restart your device.

If you think that you need to force close your Alexa application, you should go to the *Settings* section of your device. You can find that from your Home screen. Then, you should go to *Applications* or *Apps*. In some devices, however, you may still have to choose *Manage Applications* after you go to the Settings and Applications sections.

Anyway, when you are on the applications part of your settings, you have to look for the Alexa app from the list of installed apps that you have on your device. Choose *Clear Data* to remove all your application data. Finally, you have to choose *Force Stop*.

If you have to uninstall and then install the application again, you have to go to your menu, choose *Alexa*, and choose *Uninstall*. This would remove the application from your device. Then, you have to go to Google Play and get the application once more so that you can install Alexa again.

If you are using Fire OS and you wish to restart your device, you have to press down and hold the *Power* button. Then, you have to choose the option that allows you to turn off the device. When it has been turned off, you have to press down the *Power* button once more and wait for your device to restart.

If you feel the need to force close your application, you should go to the *Home* screen of your device and swipe downwards from the top. This would allow you to open the *Quick Settings*. When you are there, you have to go to *Settings OR More* and then go next to the *Apps & Games OR Applications* section. Once you are there, you have to select *Manage All Applications OR Installed Applications*.

Then, you have to search for the Alexa app on the list of installed apps on your device. When you see it, you have to choose *Clear Data*. Once you have cleared your application data, you have to choose *Force Stop*.

If you have to uninstall the app and then install it again, you have to go to your app menu, choose the Alexa app, and choose *Uninstall*. Once you have successfully uninstalled it, you need to head to the Apps library and tap on *Alexa* in order for you to get the application again. When you finally get the application, you need to install it on your device.

If you are using a Web browser, you have to reload your Web page and clear your cookies and cache. Once you are done with this step, you will see that the website settings you have previously on your browser are now gone. These settings may include your passwords and usernames. Anyway, you need to close the Web browser and then open it again in order for the changes to take effect.

Alexa Does Not See the Smart Home Device

What if your Alexa is not able to see your Smart Home device? What should you do in this case? SmartThings and Wink are two of the most commonly used smart home devices by users who also happen to have Alexa.

If your Alexa cannot find your device, you may have some issues with compatibility. This is why you need to ensure that your smart home device is really compatible with the Alexa device that you are using.

You have to obtain the companion application for the smart home device that you have. You can download it from the app store. Then, you have to set up the device. You also have to restart both the Alexa and the smart home device. Next, you have to disable and then enable your smart home skill in your Alexa application.

Finally, you have to download and install the software updates that are necessary for your devices.

How about smart home devices that do not have any skills?

WeMo and Philips smart home devices actually do not require any skill to connect with the Alexa. If you want your Alexa to discover such devices, you need to utter the word "Discover devices" if you are using a WeMo device. If you are using a Philips device, you need to press the button on the device bridge and utter the words "Discover devices."

Connecting to the Same Wi-Fi Network

Keep in mind that the Alexa device you are using have to be on the same Wi-Fi network as the smart home devices that you have. In case your Alexa device is not on a similar Wi-Fi network, you need to use your Alexa application and change the network. To do this, you have to open the application and go to the *Settings* section. You can go there by heading to the left navigation panel on your screen.

Choose the Alexa device that you have and choose *Update Wi-Fi*. You will then see a bunch of instructions on your screen. You have to follow these instructions so that you can update the Wi-Fi information.

Take note that smart home devices and the Alexa device work well on personal Wi-Fi networks. If you use public Wi-Fi networks, such as the ones in your workplace or school, your devices may not be allowed to connect with one another.

Also, you have to keep in mind that certain smart home devices are only able to connect to the 2.4 GHz Wi-Fi band. Thus, you have to verify with your smart home manufacturer and ask them questions if you have any.

If you want to turn on the SSDP / UPnP of your router, you have to call your router manufacturer. Their customer service representatives will assist you in updating the settings for your router.

You can also rename the smart home device that you have. See to it that you verify that the group name you assign your smart home device to can be easily understood by your Alexa device.

Say, the group name that you choose is "b3dr00m lights". You may want to change it to "Bedroom Lights" because it is much easier to understand. You may also name your device using the companion app of the manufacturer. If you have done this and you wish to rename it, you simply have to open the application on your mobile device and then rename it there.

When it comes to rediscovering your devices, you just have to utter the words "Discover my devices", and Alexa will confirm the beginning of your search. Once the discovery is finished, Alexa will either confirm it or tell you that it was not able to find the device.

Alexa Does Not Understand You

What if Alexa does not understand any of your requests or commands? What should you do about this issue?

In order for the Alexa to function properly, you have to have an active Wi-Fi connection. Otherwise, you will not be able to stream media or music from the cloud as well as have your requests followed or questions answered by Alexa.

See to it that you always position the Alexa device in a good location. It has to be at least eight inches away from walls or any other objects that might cause interference. Baby monitors and microwave ovens are examples of these objects. So, if you have them in your home, see to it that you do not keep them in the same room as you keep your Alexa device. In addition, it is not advisable to leave your Alexa device on your floor. You have to keep it in a higher location, such as a desk or countertop.

In order for your Alexa device to understand you, you need to speak in a loud and clear voice. Just as you would talk to a person, you need to convey your message loud and clear. See to it that there aren't any background noises whenever you speak with Alexa. You also do not have to worry about not having a good enough accent. Do not worry about your accent. Just speak clearly and naturally, and Alexa will understand you.

See to it that you are also specific with communicating with Alexa. If you have any request or question, you need to address them as specifically as possibly. Do not be vague. Just like speaking with an actual person, you do not want to be vague because you may be misunderstood or you might not get the answer that you need.

You have to refrain from making too general statements or questions. Rephrase what you say, as much as possible. For instance, if you wish to know what the weather in Springfield, Illinois is, you should say the name of the place in its entirety. You should not merely say "Springfield" because there far too many other Springfields in the world. When asking Alexa about the weather in that particular location, you can say "Alexa, what is the weather in Springfield, Illinois?" By stating the full location, Alexa is able to give you a precise answer.

You may also want to see if your Alexa app has heard you clearly. To find out about this information, go to your home screen and choose *More*, which is located at the bottom part of your interaction card. There, you will be able to read the things that your Alexa app has heard.

Using Voice Training

This feature is completely optional, and you do not have any obligation to use it. Nevertheless, if you wish to use it, you should feel free to do so. The Voice Training option is actually available to the Amazon Echo and the Amazon Tap devices. Through the Voice Training, the Alexa app is able to understand and recognize speech patterns. So, during each one of your sessions, your Alexa application shows twenty-five different phrases that you utter to the device.

The Voice Training option is actually a good idea if you want to enhance the speech recognition functionality of your Alexa device. As you say each one of the twenty-five phrases, the Alexa app processes them. In fact, it processes the words that you say even though you do not finish your session.

Nevertheless, if you are hoping to obtain the best results, see to it that you speak in a normal voice when you talk to Alexa. You should also stand or sit where you normally would whenever you speak to Alexa. In other words, you just have to do things as you normally do them. There is no need for you to change your behavior or tone of voice. If you own a voice remote, you should not use it during your Voice Training.

In order to begin your Voice Training, you need to open your Alexa application. Go to the left navigation panel that you see on your screen and choose *Settings*. Once you are there, you should choose *Voice Training* and then *Start Session*. Next, you have to utter the phrase in your Alexa application and choose *Next*.

When repeating phrases, you need to choose *Pause*. Then, you should choose *Repeat Phrase*. Once you are done with your session, you can choose *Complete*. What about if you suddenly have an emergency and you need to end the session right away? Well, you can always end your session whenever you want to. All you need to do is choose *Pause* and *End Session*.

Bluetooth Issues

Some users have reported that their mobile devices do not connect properly to their Alexa devices via Bluetooth. If you are experiencing this problem, it could be that you're having issues with compatibility. The Amazon Echo, Amazon Echo Dot, and Amazon Tap all support the Bluetooth profiles of the Advance Audio Distribution Profile or A2DP SNK and Audio / Video Remote Control Profile or AVRCP.

The Advanced Audio Distribution Profile or A2DPSNK lets you stream audio files from your mobile devices, including your tablet and mobile phone, to the Alexa device. Likewise, the Amazon Echo Dot supports this profile as well. You can stream your audio files from your Amazon Echo Dot to your Bluetooth speaker.

The Audio / Video Remote Control Profile or AVRCP lets you utilize hands-free voice control each time a mobile device connects to the Alexa device.

See to it that you always inspect the batteries of your Bluetooth device, whether such batteries are removable or not. If you have non-removable batteries, see to it that your device is fully charged. If you have replaceable batteries, you should have spare batteries that you can use once your current batteries run out of power.

See to it that you also check for interference. You have to move your Alexa device and your Bluetooth device away from any possible sources of interference, such baby monitors, microwave ovens, and various wireless devices. See to it that you also keep your Bluetooth device close to the Alexa device whenever you pair them.

Clearing Bluetooth Devices

If you are using the Amazon Echo or the Amazon Tap, just open your Alexa application. Go to the left navigation panel on your screen and choose *Settings*. Then, choose your Alexa device and choose *Bluetooth*. When you are there, you should choose the *Clear option*.

If you are using the Amazon Echo Dot, open your Alexa application and then go to the left navigation panel on your screen. Choose *Settings* and look for your Alexa device. Choose your device and then choose *Bluetooth*. Next, choose a device from your list before you choose *Forget*. You have to repeat this step for all the other Bluetooth devices that you have on your list.

Once you have cleared your devices, make sure that you restart the Alexa device as well as the Bluetooth device.

Pairing Bluetooth Devices Once More

If you are using the Amazon Echo and the Amazon Tap, just open your settings menu on your mobile device. From there, you have to turn on your *Bluetooth*. See to it that you are located near the Alexa device as you do this procedure.

Then, you have to utter the word "Pair" and make sure that your Alexa device hears your voice loud and clear. Once it does, it will go into the pairing mode. You have to go to Bluetooth settings and choose your Alexa device. Then, Alexa will inform you if your connection has been successful or not.

If you are using the Amazon Echo Dot, open your Alexa application and your left navigation panel. Choose *Settings* and search for your Alexa device. Choose *Bluetooth* and then choose *Pair a New Device*. Once you do this, the Alexa device will then go into the pairing mode. Next, open your Bluetooth settings and choose your Alexa device. You will then be informed whether your connection is successful or not.

Issues with Regard to Streaming on the Alexa Device

It really sucks when you are trying to listen to your favorite song or audio book but your Alexa device won't cooperate. This simple issue can ruin your trip or even your day. So, what can you do about it?

Well, you should take note that an intermittent connection or low bandwidth can cause streaming problems. This is why you need to make sure that you have a good Internet connection. If you want to stream audiobooks, music, and other content via the Alexa device, you need to have an Internet connection that is at least 512 Kbps or 0.51 Mbps.

If you are running several devices on a Wi-Fi network all at once, you may also experience issues with regard to performance. So, if you want to solve this issue, you have to turn off the devices that you are not using. Doing so will free up some of the bandwidth on the network.

You also have to move your device much closer to the modem and router if possible. Sometimes, performance issues exist because the device is located in another room or the connection is blocked.

You have already heard this tip before, but remember it at all times: always keep your Alexa device away from metal objects, walls, and other possible sources of interference, such as baby monitors and microwave ovens. It is also not a good idea to leave your Alexa device on your floor. You have to move it up to a higher ground or location. You can keep it on your shelf, table, or wherever as long as the location is stable and away from sources of interference.

The Amazon Echo and the Amazon Echo Dot Connect to the 5 GHz Channel of the Router

A lot of Wi-Fi devices solely connect to the 2 GHz channel. So, if there are several devices that make use of this channel in your network, you may experience a slower network speed. If you are on a dual-band router, you may connect the Amazon Echo to a less congested 5 GHz channel in order for you to get much less interference and a better range.

Restarting the Alexa and the Network Hardware

This can help you solve your issues with your Wi-Fi – and this usually does. If you want to restart properly, just turn off the modem and the router. Then, wait for about thirty seconds before you turn on the modem. Wait for it to restart and then turn on the router next. Again, just wait for it to restart. When your devices have restarted, you have to turn off your Alexa device and then turn it on once more.

How about if you are still experiencing issues after you have done these steps? If you have already done the steps mentioned above and yet you are still not able to use your device properly, you may have to call your router manufacturer, network administrator, or Internet service provider.

Downloading the Amazon Alexa Application

The Alexa is an awesome application that you can download for free. It can help you manage your shopping list, to-do lists, music, alarms, and so much more! Then again, you have to keep in mind that this application is only currently available in the United States. So, if you are outside of the country, you will not be able to download it. In addition, this application is not supported by the Kindle Fire first and second generations.

Anyway, you can download the Amazon Alexa application from the Apple App Store, Google Play, and the Amazon App Store. If you want to check for updates, go to your app store and look for the Alexa app. When you see an available update, all you have to do is tap on Update and wait for your app to be updated. On the other hand, if you do not see any available updates, there is no need to panic because it only means that you have the most recent version of the application.

The Amazon Alexa Application Basics

If this is your first time to use the Alexa application, you'll want to read further below to learn about its fundamentals. You can actually use the application on most electronic devices, including your computer and mobile phone.

The Home Screen

The Alexa application features a Home screen in which you can view your activities using the device. You have to scroll through the "Cards" on your Home scree in order for you to view the descriptions of your most recent requests and activities. You can also see the other features available, such as an option to get rid of the card or give feedback.

The Left Navigation Panel

In order for you to open your left navigation panel, you have to choose the Menu icon on your Alexa application. You will then see the settings and features that you have on your Alexa device. Keep in mind that whenever you view the application on your computer, you already have your left navigation panel opened.

So, what options can you see on the Menu section of your application?

You will see Home, which allows you to see your most recent interactions with the Alexa application.

You will see Now Playing, which allows you to see and take control of the tracks that play on your device. It also allows you to view any upcoming tracks in your queue, as well as check out your history.

You will see Music and Books, which allows you to search for songs, shows, stations, audio books, and Kindle e-books that you want to listen to on your device.

You will see Shopping and To-Do Lists, which allows you to see and manage both your to-do and shopping lists.

You will see Timers and Alarms, which allows you to see and take control of your alarms and timers.

You will see Skills, which allows you to search for and turn on the skills that add a variety of voice-driven capabilities to the device.

You will see Smart Home, which allows you to manage your smart home devices that are connected to Alexa.

You will see Things to Try, which allows you to check out a list of sample phrases that you may say to your Alexa device.

You will see Settings, which allows you to set up your device and train it to understand and recognize your speech patterns. It also makes the device adjust to your settings.

You will see Help and Feedback, which allows you to seek help in case you need it. It also allows you to give feedback with regard to your user experience with the Alexa device.

You will see Not [NAME] ? Sign out, which allows you to sign out of the application when you are done using it.

It is important to take note that you are only allowed to sign out of the application when you are on a Web browser, iOS, or Android. If you are using an Android device, signing out of the Alexa application automatically logs you out from other Amazon applications, such as the Kindle application, that you have on your device.

Settings of the Amazon Alexa Application

You have to familiarize yourself with the settings involved in the Alexa application so that you can easily change and update them. Then again, you have to keep in mind that certain settings may not be available or applicable to your device.

For instance, there is the Battery. This setting is only available for Amazon Tap. So, if you are using the Amazon Echo or the Amazon Echo Dot, this setting is not applicable to your device. The Battery checks your current battery level.

The Connect to Wi-Fi / Update Wi-Fi setting sets up or updates the Wi-Fi network that you have.

The Bluetooth setting changes the pairing options for Bluetooth that you have on your device.

The Pair / Forget remote setting is only available for the Amazon Echo and the Amazon Echo Dot. It either pairs or unpairs the remote for the Echo and the Echo Dot.

The Sounds setting manages the sounds or audio files that you have on your device when you interact with it.

The Device name setting allows you to give your device a new name. This setting is actually highly useful if you have a lot of Alexa devices in your office or home. Assigning different names to your Alexa devices prevents confusion and misunderstanding. To change the name of your device, you simply have to enter the name on the name field and then choose Save Changes.

The Device Location setting adds your address to your device. The Alexa application then makes use of this information to provide you with updates regarding the weather, time, movie schedules, or nearby restaurants. See to it that you input your correct address. You have to enter the name of your street, your city, state, and finally your ZIP code on the field. Then, choose Save.

The Wake Word setting is only applicable to the Amazon Echo and the Amazon Echo Dot. It manages your choice of a wake word. On certain Alexa devices, this word determines the way you initiate your voice requests with Alexa.

The Metric Measurements setting makes use of metric measurements for distance and temperature units.

The Device Is Registered To: setting lets you view the present registration status of your device. If you wish to deregister the device, you simply have to choose Deregister.

The Device Software Version setting is about the current software version you have on your device.

The Serial Number setting is actually the serial number of your device.

The MAC Address setting is actually the MAC address of your device.

How about account settings?

The Voice Training setting trains the Alexa device to understand and recognize your voice better.

The Music and Media setting connects a compatible media or music service to your device.

The Flash Briefing setting chooses shows, weather updates, and headlines for your Flash Briefing.

The Traffic setting uses information about your location to come up with travel time estimates whenever you travel somewhere.

The Calendar setting connects your Google Calendar account with Alexa in order to find out about any upcoming events.

The Smart Home setting connects smart home devices that are compatible with the Alexa device as well as allows it to take control of these products whenever you ask.

The Voice Purchasing setting enables you to order physical products and digital music from the Amazon website using your voice. As a security measure, it also enables the optional confirmation code that the Alexa asks you to mention before you place your orders.

The Household Profiles setting lets you create and join the Amazon Household, so you can listen to the content from various Amazon accounts.

The About the Amazon Alexa App setting lets you check out the most recent version of the Alexa application.

Changing Your Alexa Device Location

The Alexa device relies on the location of your device when it comes up with answers to your questions with regard to time, weather, local searches, and local features.

If you wish to change your Alexa device location, you simply have to open your left navigation panel and choose *Settings*. Then, you have to search for your device. While you are in the *Device location* section, you have to choose *Edit* and then input your complete address. Review what you have entered and if you are absolutely sure about the information that you provided, you have to save it by choosing *Save*.

In case you have several Alexa devices, see to it that you update the locations of each one of the devices.

Household Profiles on the Alexa Devices

Through the Household Profiles, you are able to add another person to your Amazon Household and listen to each other's content. This is great because you can share audio books and music files. You can also manage shared features, such as lists. What's more, you can share content purchases with the other member across other media applications and devices.

Then again, you have to keep in mind that when you add another person into your Household, you are also giving authority to that person to use the credit cards that you have on your Amazon account. In other words, this other person has access to your credit cards and is legitimately authorized to make purchases on the site using your credit cards.

If you wish to gain more security, you may set up a four-digit code and have it required to be stated aloud each time something is bought online using your credit card. To set up this confirmation code, choose *Settings* from your Alexa application and then choose *Voice Purchasing*.

Adding and Removing Users to Your Household

When you add another user to your household, it is necessary for this other person to be present in the room with you because he has to input his account information. Anyway, when you are on your left navigation panel, you have to choose *Settings* and then *Account*. Next, you have to choose *Household Profile* and simply follow the instructions you see on the screen.

If you wish to remove a user from your Household, you have to take note that you cannot add both user accounts to a new Household for one hundred and eighty days. So, if you removed a user by accident and you want to add him to your Household again, you have to call Customer Support and ask for assistance.

Anyway, if you really want to remove the user from your Household, you have to go to your left navigation panel and choose *Settings*. Then, you have to choose *Household Profile* under *Account*. Next, you have to choose *Remove* to remove the user. If you wish to remove yourself from the Household, you have to choose *Leave*. Finally, you have to choose *Remove from Household* in order to confirm the changes that you have just made.

Switching to Another Profile

Once you are done setting up your Household, you are free to switch accounts between the users on your Alexa device. To do this, you have to say the words "Switch accounts." If you are browsing through a content library in your Alexa application, you can use the drop-down menu, which can be found at the top portion of your screen. This would allow you to toggle between the user libraries. If you wish to check the profile that you are using at present, you simply have to say the words "Which account is this?"

Enabling Alexa Skills

The Alexa device feature skills, which are voice-driven capabilities that improve its functionality. As the user, you are free to choose which skills you want to be enabled. For instance, you may enable skills that will make the device play games with you or inform you about the latest happenings in your area.

In order for you to use the Alexa skills, you have to enable them in your application. Then, you have to make a request based on the sample phrases that you have in the application.

If you know exactly what skill you want to be enabled, you simply have to say "Enable (skill name) skill". In addition, you can search for the skill in the application and enable it there.

To do this, open the application and go to the left navigation panel. Then, choose *Skills*. You can use the search bar to input your keywords or choose *Categories* and browse through the skill categories present. Once you spotted the skill that you wish to use, you have to choose *Enable Skill*.

Once you successfully enabled this skill, you may request for Alexa to open the skill and use it. For instance, you may command Alexa by saying "Alexa, open (skill name). Take note that there may be additional or different instructions related to using these skills.

You may refer to the detail page of the skill in your application if you want to find out more about it. You may also ask Alexa to help you out by saying "Alexa, (skill name) help." If you do not want to use a particular skill anymore, simply because you are tired or bored with it or you do not need it anymore, you can disable it by choosing *Disable* or commanding Alexa to disable the skill.

As a user, you are allowed to review and rate skills. In order for you to review a certain skill, you have to

scroll downwards to Reviews and choose *Write a Review*.

Sending Feedback Regarding the Alexa

Users are actually encouraged to send their feedback to the developers so that the Alexa can be improved. When you send feedback through the application, however, it contains certain diagnostic information.

Anyway, if you want to send your feedback, open the application and go to your left navigation panel. Choose *Help and Feedback* and then *Send Feedback.* You can search for your device using the drop-down menu. You can use the same menu to search for your chosen category and issue type. Then, you will see a text box in which you can write your comments, issues, or suggestions with regard to the Alexa. When you are done, you just have to hit *Send Feedback.*

Viewing the Dialog History

If you want to see a transcript and even listen to your interactions with Alexa, you can go to your *Dialog History.* Here, you can even delete or remove certain recordings that you do not want to exit anymore.

In order for you to listen to the dialog history, you have to open the application and choose *Settings* from your left navigation panel. Then, you have to choose History. You will be presented with a list of interactions. You can choose which interaction you want to listen to. Click on it and choose *Play.*

If you want to delete individual recordings, you have to choose *Delete Voice Recordings.* By doing so, you also remove the audio files that are streamed on the Cloud. Similarly, you remove the Home screen cards that are associated with the interaction. However, if you just want to remove the Home screen cards in the application, you can go to the Home screen and choose *Remove Card.*

If you want to delete all of the interactions that you have made with Alexa, you have to choose *Manage Your Content and Device.* Then, you have to choose *Your Devices* so that you can see the list of the devices registered on your account. From there, you can choose your device. Finally, you have to choose *Manage Voice Recordings* and *Delete.*

Chapter 4: Amazon Echo Issues

The Amazon Echo is a fascinating and useful device, but it is not perfect. Even though it is great, there are still certain issues involved with it.

The Amazon Echo Remote Issues

If the remote feature of your Amazon Echo is not successfully pairing or working with your device, you may be having some compatibility or battery issues. In this case, you need to check for compatibility and ensure that you have working batteries.

Keep in mind that the voice remote is only compatible with the Amazon Echo and the Amazon Echo Dot. Therefore, you cannot use it with any other Alexa-enabled devices, such as the Amazon Fire TV and the Amazon Tap.

If compatibility is not the problem, perhaps it is the batteries. Take note that batteries may sometimes lose their charge if they have been sitting out there for too long. If this is the case, you have to insert a couple of new AAA batteries into your remote and test it out. When you insert the batteries, see to it that they are in their proper orientations.

To see if your issue has been resolved, you have to pair your remote again. This time, you have to move your Amazon Echo device closer to you. Open your left navigation panel in your application and choose *Settings*. Choose your Amazon Echo device and choose *Pair Remote*. If you see *Forget Remote* in your application, it means that you already have a remote paired with the device. You can choose Forget Remote if you want to replace the remote that you are currently using.

Press down and hold the *Play / Pause* button on your remote for about five seconds in order to begin the pairing process. Your device will search for the remote and then connect with it in forty seconds. Sometimes, though, it takes longer than forty seconds to successfully connect the device. Once your device finds the remote, Alexa will inform you that your remote has already been paired. When this happens, you can press down the talk button on your remote and verify if Alexa can finally respond.

Restarting the Device

If you have followed the steps mentioned above and still you fail to get your desired results, you may have to restart the device. All you have to do is disconnect your power adapter from the power outlet or the back of your device, and then plug it back into your device. When your device restarts, you can begin to pair the remote again. See to it that you continue to press down and hold the *Play / Pause* button as you pair your remote. You have to keep doing this until Alexa tells you that your remote has successfully paired.

Resetting the Amazon Echo

If your Amazon Echo device is not responding to your commands, questions, or requests, you may have to reset it. Likewise, if you wish to give the device to a family member or friend, you also have to reset it so that new information can be stored in it. Once the Amazon Echo has been reset, it has to be registered with an Amazon account and any device settings used for it have to re-entered.

If you are having some issues with your Amazon Echo, you have to restart it first in order to see if your issues can be resolved. To restart the device, unplug its power adapter from its back or from a wall outlet, and then plug it back in.

To reset the Amazon Echo, use a paper clip or any other similar item to press down and hold the *Reset* button for approximately five seconds. The *Reset* button is actually located at the bottom part of the device. Once you press down and hold this button, you will see the light ring on the device turning orange and blue, respectively.

You have to wait for the light ring to be off and then on once more. When the light ring becomes orange, your Amazon Echo device goes into the setup mode. You have to open your application to connect the device with a Wi-Fi network as well as register it with an Amazon account.

The Amazon Echo Device Does Not Connect to a Wi-Fi Network

As you have read in previous chapters, you need to have a Wi-Fi connection in order to use the Amazon Echo. Once again, it is worth noting that the Amazon Echo device connects to a dual-band Wi-Fi (2.4 GHz / 5 GHz) network that uses the 802.11 a/b/g/n standard. The Amazon Echo does not support any peer-to-peer or ad-hoc network.

Checking the Status of Your Wi-Fi Network

You can find out about the current status of your Wi-Fi network when you check the power LED on your device. The power LED is located near the power adapter port.

The solid white light states that your Amazon Echo is connected to a Wi-Fi network. On the other hand, the solid orange light indicates that your Amazon Echo is not connected to a Wi-Fi network. The blinking orange light states that your Amazon Echo is connected to a Wi-Fi network, but is not able to gain access to the Alexa Voice Service.

If you are experiencing any issues, you can try to connect again to the Wi-Fi network. See to it that you know exactly what your password is. Then again, a password is not always required. You can go without it. If you notice a lock icon, it means that there is a required password. Keep in mind that this password is certainly not your password for your Amazon account.

Make sure that you also verify if the other devices you have, including your mobile phones and tablets, are able to connect to the network. Otherwise, you may have more problems with the Wi-Fi network. If this is the case, you have to call your Internet service provider or network administrator for help.

You also have to update your firmware for the modem or router. If you have any saved Wi-Fi password in your Amazon account, but you have just changed it, you have to input your new Wi-Fi password again in order to reconnect.

Reducing Wi-Fi Congestion

At times, inconsistent Wi-Fi is noticed if there are a variety of devices connected to the Wi-Fi network.

If this is the case, you need to turn off some of your devices, particularly the ones that you are not using. You need to do this in order to free up some network bandwidth. Then, you have to move your device and position it closer to your modem or router.

Restarting the Amazon Echo Device and the Network Hardware

You may restart your Amazon Echo device, modem, and router to solve your Wi-Fi issues.

To do this, you have to turn off the modem and router, and then wait for about thirty seconds. Then, you have to turn on the modem and wait for it to restart. Once your modem has been restarted, you have to turn on the router and wait for it to restart as well.

As you wait for your network hardware to restart, you have to unplug your power adapter for about three seconds and then plug it in again. After you have restarted your Amazon Echo and network hardware, you can attempt to connect to the Wi-Fi network once more.

If you are still having issues despite following the instructions stated above, you should contact your network administrator, Internet service provider, or router manufacturer to ask for assistance.

Chapter 5: Fun Things to Try with Alexa

Having Alexa to keep you company is truly loads of fun. If you have just gotten your device, however, you may be wondering what activities you can do with it. Well, here are some of the things that you might want to try with Alexa.

The Daily Show

If you are a fan of The Daily Show with Trevor Noah, you will be glad to know that Alexa can provide you with a good dose of the show on a regular basis. You can listen to clips from recent episodes or learn about the guest list. All you have to do is ask Alexa. You can say "Alexa, ask The Daily Show for news" or "Alexa, enable The Daily Show skill".

Washington Post Election News

If you are interested in news related to the White House elections, you can ask Alexa to give you poll data. You can say "Alexa, ask WaPo Elections for the polls" or "Alexa, ask WaPo Elections for the Politics Brief".

Game of Thrones Quotes

Who has not heard of the popular TV show Game of Thrones? If you love the show and can't get enough of it, you can ask Alexa to give you quotes. Just say: "Alexa, give me a Game of Thrones quote". You can also ask Alexa some trivia about the show. For instance, you can ask her who the Mother of Dragons is or what the words of the House Stark are.

Local News Updates in Flash Briefing

If you are interested to know about your local news updates, you can modify your Flash Briefing. You can choose from a variety of metropolitan news sources. Once you have taken your pick, you can ask Alexa what your Flash Briefing is. You can say "Alexa, what is my Flash Briefing?"

You can actually get a tip from Alexa every day. You just have to add Alexa Things to Try on your Flash Briefing sources list.

Tracking Packages

Amazon is such a great place to shop for items. If you ordered something and are expecting to get it, you can ask Alexa to track your package for you. There is no more need for you to go online or make a phone call. Alexa will tell you exactly when your package is going to arrive. It will also inform you when you placed your order as well as include a link that contains more details in your application. You can find out about all of this by asking Alexa to help you out. You can say "Alexa, track my order" or "Alexa, where's my stuff?"

Adding Calendar Events Using Your Voice

Now, you can ask Alexa to organize your Google Calendar for you. You can add events using your voice by going to Setting and tapping on Calendar. When you are done setting up, you can ask Alexa to add events to your calendar. You can say "Alexa, add an event to my calendar". You can also add specific events. For instance, you can say "Alexa, add 'brunch with Mom' to my calendar."

Setting Alarms

Alexa can also function as your alarm clock. Yes, you can set it to go off at the same time every day. You can even have a particular alarm for the weekdays and another one for the weekends. For instance, you can say "Alexa, set an alarm for every Sunday at 10 A.M." or "Alexa, set a repeating alarm for weekdays at 8."

Chapter 6: Music and Media

You are free to select which service you want Alexa to use to play your music and follow your commands.

In your application, you need to open your left navigation panel and choose Settings. Then, you have to choose Music & Media and Choose default music services. Feel free to select a default music library, such as Spotify or Amazon Music, as well as a default station service, such as iHeartRadio, Pandora, or Amazon Music. Once you are done choosing the services that you like, you can choose Done.

Listening to Music and Media

Alexa is useful for a lot of things, including streaming podcasts, audio books, and music among others from your mobile device, via Bluetooth, or from a streaming service provider. You are also allowed to upload music collections from iTunes and Google Play Music to your Amazon music library and play them using your device.

Alexa actually supports a number of subscription-based and free streaming services, such as Amazon Music, Spotify Premium, Prime Music, Audible, iHeartRadio, TuneIn, and Pandora.

You can request for Alexa to stream live radio, music, podcasts, and audio books directly from these streaming services to your device. You need to register your Alexa device with your Amazon account, though. Once you are done with the process, you can gain access to the music and audiobooks in your libraries. If you are a Prime member, you can enjoy more stations, playlists, and songs via Prime Music.

Uploading Music

If you want to play your music from Google Play or iTunes on your device, you may use the Amazon Music for Mac and PC to upload music collections from your computer to your Amazon music library. You are allowed to upload up to two hundred and fifty songs for free.

If you want to upload more songs, you have to get an Amazon Music subscription. If you do, you will be able to upload up to two hundred and fifty thousand songs. Then again, any purchase you make from the Digital Music Store does not count to the two hundred and fifty song limit.

Anyway, when you are done uploading your music, you may request Alexa to play it. You can also control the playback by using simple voice commands.

Streaming Media and Music via Bluetooth

The Amazon Echo, the Amazon Echo Dot, and the Amazon Tap all support the Advanced Audio Distribution Profile or A2DP. So, you can stream audio via Bluetooth. These devices also support the Audio / Video Remote Control Profile or AVRCP, which is meant for the voice control of connected devices.

Linking Third-Party Music Services to Alexa

If you want to listen to streaming music, you may have to link your account in Pandora, iHeartRadio, or Spotify Premium to your Alexa device.

To do this, you have to open your left navigation panel in your Alexa application and choose Music & Books. Then, you have to choose your streaming music service. When you are done with that, you have to choose Link Account to Alexa. You will then see a sign-in page on the screen. You have to sign in using your email and password.

In case you encounter any error messages as you attempt to connect your account with Alexa, you just have to reset the username and password that you are using for your streaming service. Then, you should attempt to connect your account with Alexa again.

Keep in mind that your use of streaming music services might be subject to added charges, depending on the policy of your streaming service. Do not worry, though. You can always unlink Alexa from your streaming music service any time you want. You just have to choose Unlike Account from Alexa from your Alexa application.

Basic Music Commands

You can use Alexa to listen to music as well. It's pretty easy – intuitive, even. You just have to utter the right commands.

For instance, if you want to adjust the volume of your music, you have to say "Set volume to level (number)" , "Volume up" , or "Volume down".

If you want to learn more about the details of the track you are currently listening to, you can say "Who is this?" , "What is this?" , "Who is this artist?" , or "What song is this?"

If you no longer want to listen to music and you want the track to be stopped, you just have to say "Stop" or "Pause", and Alexa will stop playing the music.

On the other hand, if are in the mood for a song, you can command Alexa to start playing one by saying "Play". If you have been listening to a song and you paused it, but now you want it to be played again, you can say "Resume".

If you are using a sleep timer, you can either set it up or cancel it. You can say "Set a sleep timer for (x) minutes" or "Stop playing music in (x) minutes". You can also say "Cancel sleep timer".

What about if you want to go back to a previous track or you want to skip a track and listen to the next one? This is easy. You just have to say "Previous" or "Next", and Alexa will go back or move forward.

If you want to loop your music queue, you can simply say "Loop". If you want to shuffle the songs in your playlist, you can say "Shuffle". Conversely, if you wish to stop shuffling, you can say "Stop shuffle". If you want to play a particular song again, you can say "Repeat".

Advanced Music Commands

Of course, if there are basic commands, there are also advanced commands. Alexa is much more intelligent than you may have thought.

If you want to play a song, you can say "Play the song (name of song)" or "Play some music". If you want to play a certain album, you can say "Play the album (name of album).

If you want to play songs according to genre, artist, or playlist, you can also tell that to Alexa. You can say "Play songs by (name of artist)" , "Play some (name of genre) music" , "Play some (

name of genre) music from Prime" , "Shuffle my (name of playlist) playlist" , or "Listen to my (name of playlist) playlist".

If you like a particular song from Pandora, Prime, or iHeartRadio, you can say "Thumbs up" or "I like this song". If you do not like it, you can say "Thumbs down" or "I don't like this song".

You can also remove a certain song from the rotation by saying "I'm tired of this song". This only applies to Prime and Pandora, however. If you want to create a station in Pandora or iHeartRadio, you can say "Create an iHeartRadio station based on (artist)" or "Make a station for (artist)".

Selecting Music Service Preferences

If you want to select which services you want Alexa to use to play music, you have to open your left navigation panel, choose Settings, choose Music & Media, and choose Choose Default Music Services. You are allowed to select a default music library, such as Spotify or Amazon Music, as well as a default station service, such as iHeartRadio, Amazon Music, or Pandora. When you are done choosing your preferred services, you can hit Done.

Listening to Audio Books

You can play audio books from Kindle Unlimited and Audible in your Alexa device. Even more good news, the Whispersync for Voice is supported by Alexa. As you know, it tracks your current playback positions in your audio books. You can begin to listen to your audio book, stop for a while, and then go back to listening to it. You just have to read or listen to the same title on another device or application that is compatible with it.

Unfortunately, the Alexa doesn't support narration speed control, bookmarks, notes, stats, badges, newspaper audios, and magazine audios.

Anyway, when listening to an audio book, you can command Alexa to read or play for you by saying "Read (title)" , "Play the book (title)" , "Play (title) from Audible" , or "Play the audio book (title).

If you want to pause your audio book, you simply have to utter "Pause". If you want to resume listening to it, you just have to say "Resume my book".

You can also go forward or backwards in your audio book by thirty seconds. You can say "Go back" or "Go forward". Likewise, if you want to go back or forward to a chapter, you can say "Previous chapter" or "Next chapter".

If you wish to go to a particular chapter, you can say "Go to chapter (number of chapter)". You can even restart the chapter by saying "Restart". Furthermore, you can set up or cancel a sleep timer for your audio book. You can say "Set a sleep timer for (x) minutes" , "Stop reading the book in (x) minutes" or "Cancel sleep timer".

Reading Kindle Books

You can also read Kindle books using Alexa. Alexa will read them to us using the same text-to-speech technology used for calendar events, Wikipedia articles, and news articles.

Alexa can read books that are borrowed from Kindle Unlimited or Kindle Owners' Lending Library, as well as books that are bought from the Kindle Store. Alexa can also read shared books in your Family Library.

Unfortunately, Alexa doesn't support narration speed control as well as comics and graphic novels in Kindle.

To search for eligible books in your Alexa application, just open your left navigation panel and choose Music & Books. Then, you should choose Kindle Books and Books Alexa Can Read.

Whenever you ask Alexa to read a book, it picks up from wherever you left off in the book on another reading application or device that is compatible with it. If you want read different chapters in your book, you can choose Now Playing from your Alexa application and then choose Queue. Then, you will be presented with a list that contains the chapters of your book.

Chapter 7: News, Weather, and Traffic

You have heard about Flash Briefing from previous chapters. With it, Alexa gives you pre-recorded updates from well-known broadcasters, including the Economists, NPR, and BBC News. You also get to know about the latest headlines and weather reports from The Associated Press and AccuWeather, respectively.

If you are a sports enthusiast, you can learn about the latest sports updates by asking Alexa about upcoming games or scores of your favorite teams. Just make sure that you add your favorite sports team under Sports Update in your Alexa application. You are allowed to add up to fifteen teams.

Some of the supported leagues are as follows: Major League Baseball (MLB) , Major League Soccer (MLS) , National Basketball Association (NBA) , English Premier League (EPL), National Collegiate Athletic Association (NCAA men's basketball), National Football League (NFL), National Collegiate Athletic Association: Football Bowl Subdivision (NCAA FBS football) , National Hockey League (NHL) , and Women's National Basketball Association (WNBA).

In order for you to add your chosen teams, you have to open your Alexa application, go to your left navigation panel, choose Settings, and go to Sports Update. Then, you have to enter the name of your chosen team into the given search field. Do not worry because you will be given suggestions, in case you forgot the name of the team. You have to select a team to add to your Sports Update.

If you wish to remove a certain team, you just have to click on the "x" located beside the name of the team. Whenever you want to hear updates about your favorite teams, you can say "Give me my Sports Update" to Alexa.

Checking Weather Forecasts

Alexa is also reliable when it comes to giving local weather forecasts. You can even find out about the weather forecasts in international cities.

First of all, you have to add your address in your Alexa application. You have read about this step from a previous chapter. When you are done with that, you can ask Alexa about the weather. Every time you do this, a card shows up in your Alexa application. It contains the weather forecast of your desired location for the entire seven days of the week. Alexa relies on AccuWeather for its weather reports.

Checking Traffic

Once you have set your starting and ending points in your Alexa application, Alexa will inform you about the traffic condition of your commute. You can rely on Alexa to give you an estimated duration of your travel. You can even ask Alexa to provide you with the quickest route.

First, you need to input your commute data. You have to open the left navigation panel in your Alexa application, choose Settings, and then choose Traffic. Then, choose Change Address from the From and To sections. You have to input a starting point as well as a destination address in the sections. When you are done with that, you have to choose Save Changes.

If you wish to add another stop in your route, you have to choose Add Stop. However, you are only allowed to add one more stop.

If you are curious about the traffic situation in your area, you can ask Alexa about it. You can say "How is traffic?" , "What's traffic like right now?" , or "What's my commute?".

Searching for Places Nearby

If you are in search of a good restaurant, boutique, or any other establishment, you can ask Alexa. You need to input your address in your Alexa application because Alexa will rely on this. Then, you just have to sit back, relax, and wait for Alexa to inform you about the best restaurants, bars, and hangouts in town.

Finding Movie Showtimes

How about movies? Can Alexa help you buy a ticket? Well, Alexa cannot book the ticket for you, but it can tell you about the movies that are playing in nearby theatres. In fact, you can even find out about the movies that are playing in the next city.

You just have to input your address and location into your Alexa application. Alexa relies on the information provided by IMDb. Whatever information it gets regarding movies and theatres, it relays this information to you. If you want to know more about such movies, you can check out your Alexa application for their ratings.

Ask Alexa

If you want to know about something or you are just plain bored, you can talk to Alexa. You can ask random questions and be surprised at the answers. Alexa is actually capable of answering questions related to people, dates, geography, sports, music, dates, and more! It can also define words, spell, make simple calculations, and complete conversations. How about if Alexa was not able to answer a particular question? Well, if this happens, you can use your application to send feedback to the developers.

Chapter 8: Shopping

Amazon is best known as an online marketplace. It is the go-to place for many people who want to buy new clothes, shoes, accessories, furniture, gadgets, or home décor.

You can actually ask Alexa to order Prime-eligible products for you. However, before you can place an order, you need to get a thirty-day free trial or annual Amazon Prime membership. You also need to have a billing address in the United States, a payment method, and a 1-Click payment method.

The shipping address and payment method that you indicated in your 1-Click are the ones that Alexa will use whenever you order something. In addition, you have to keep in mind that the orders you place for any physical product are eligible for free returns.

Anyway, if you want to buy a Prime-eligible item, you can say "Alexa, order a (name of item)" or simply a "Yes" or a "No" whenever Alexa finds a product and asks you if you want to confirm your order.

If you wish to reorder a particular item, you can say "Reorder (name of item)" or just a "Yes" or a "No". If you want to add an item to your Amazon cart, you can say "Add (name of item) to my cart" and Alexa will do just that.

You can also track the status of your order by saying "Track my order" or "Where is my stuff?". If you wish to cancel your order right after you placed it, you just have to say "Cancel my order".

Then again, in the event that Alexa was not able to cancel your order, you can cancel it yourself by managing your order at Your Orders. Also, you can change the shopping settings in your Alexa application by requiring a confirmation code. You have read about this from a previous chapter.

Purchasing Music

If you want to purchase music, you can go to the Digital Music Store. The purchases you make are stored for free in your Amazon Music library. They do not count against your storage limits, and they are available for download or playback on a compatible device that you register to your account in Amazon. If you are a Prime member, you can even add Prime Music to your library for free.

Anyway, if you want to shop for a particular album or song, you can say "Shop for the album (name of album) " or "Shop for the song (name of song)". You can also shop for songs according to artists. You can say "Shop for new songs by (name of artist)" or "Shop for songs by (name of artist)".

When buyers search for songs to buy, sample music is usually played to entertain them and to promote the music. If you like the sample music that is playing, you can purchase it by saying "Buy this song" , "Buy this album" , "Add this song to my library" , or "Add this album to my library". Alexa will notify you in case your item does not come with additional costs for Prime Music.

Purchasing Physical Products

Of course, physical products are the most popular products on the Amazon website. You can ask Alexa to choose Prime-eligible products. However, some items are not available for voice purchasing. These items include clothes, shoes, watches, and jewelry. Amazon Fresh, Add-On items, Prime Now, and Prime Pantry are also not eligible.

Each time you make a purchase using your voice, Alexa looks through a variety of purchase options, including your Order History, Amazon's Choice, and Prime-eligible items from Amazon.

Alexa will inform you of the name and the price of the item if it is available. Then, it will ask you to either cancel or confirm your order. In case Alexa is not able to find the item that you want or it cannot complete your purchase request, it may give you alternative options, such as adding an item to your cart or shopping list.

Turning Off Purchasing

If you want to turn off purchasing, you can go to Settings and then Voice Purchasing. Then, you can change your settings and turn this functionality off.

Alexa is indeed useful and fun. However, if you are not satisfied with its current state, don't worry because it is guaranteed to improve over time. The developers designed Alexa to get better as time passes by. It makes use of your voice recordings and other vital information, including the ones coming from your third-party services. Alexa processes every information you feed it. The more you use it, the more it gets to know you.

Conclusion

I hope this book was able to help you learn more about the Amazon Echo and Alexa, as well as how to use them properly. The next step is to apply the methods that you have learned from this book so that you can make the most of your new device.

I wish you the best of luck!

To your success,

William Seals

Made in the USA
Middletown, DE
31 October 2016